SHORT WALKS SHETLAND ISLANDS

by Graham Uney

Walkers heading over the tombolo to St Ninian's Isle

CONTENTS

Using this guide 4
Route summary table 6
Map key 7
Introduction 9
  Walking on Shetland 9
  Special things to see 10
  Bases and places to stay 11
  Getting there and around 12

The walks
  Walk 1. Lerwick town trail 13
  Walk 2. Bressay: The Ward of Bressay 19
  Walk 3. West Burra: Kettla Ness 23
  Walk 4. St Ninian's Isle 31
  Walk 5. Scat Ness and the Ness of Burgi 35
  Walk 6. Sumburgh Head and Jarlshof 41
  Walk 7. Drongi Field from Westerwick 49
  Walk 8. The Broch of Culswick 55
  Walk 9. Staneydale Temple 59
  Walk 10. Sandness Hill from Huxter 63
  Walk 11. Muckle Roe and the Hole of Hellier 71
  Walk 12. Grind of the Navir and Eshaness 75
  Walk 13. Ronas Hill from Collafirth Hill 81
  Walk 14. Unst: Framgord 85
  Walk 15. Unst: Hermaness 89

Useful information 94

USING THIS GUIDE

Routes in this book

In this book you will find a selection of easy or moderate walks suitable for almost everyone, including casual walkers and families with children, or for when you only have a short time to fill. The routes have been carefully chosen to allow you to explore the area and its attractions. Most routes are circular or out-and-back, although some linear walks may be included that use public transport to get back to the start. Although there may be some climbs there is no challenging terrain, but do bear in mind that conditions can sometimes be wet or muddy underfoot. A route summary table is included on page 6 to help you choose the right walk.

Clothing and footwear

You won't need any special equipment to enjoy these walks. The weather in Britain can be changeable, so choose clothing suitable for the season and wear or carry a waterproof jacket. For footwear, comfortable walking boots or trainers with a good grip are best. A small rucksack for drinks, snacks and spare clothing is useful. See www.adventuresmart.uk.

Walk descriptions

At the beginning of each walk you'll find all the information you need:

- start/finish location, with postcode and a what3words address to help you find it
- parking and transport information, estimated walking time, total distance and climb
- details of public toilets available along the route and where you can get refreshments
- a summary of the key highlights of the walk and what you might see

Timings given are the time to complete the walk at a reasonable walking pace. Allow extra time for extended stops or if walking with children.

The route is described in clear, easy-to-follow directions, with each waypoint marked on an accompanying map extract. It's a good idea to read the whole of the route instructions before setting out, so that you know what to expect.

Maps, GPX files and what3words

Extracts from the OS® 1:25,000 map accompany each route. GPX files for all the walks in this book are available to download at www.cicerone.co.uk/1194/gpx.

What3words is a free smartphone app which identifies every 3m square of the globe with a unique three-word address, e.g. ///destiny.cafe.sonic. For more information see https://what3words.com/products/what3words-app.

USING THIS GUIDE

Walking with children

Even young children can be surprisingly strong walkers, but every family is different and you may need to adapt the timings given in this book to take that into account. Make sure you go at the pace of the slowest member and choose a walk with an exciting objective in mind, such as a cave, river, waterfall or picnic spot. Many of the walks can be shortened to suit – suggestions are included at the end of the route description.

Dogs

Sheep or cattle may be found grazing on a number of these walks. Keep dogs under control at all times so that they don't scare or disturb livestock or wildlife. Cattle, particularly cows with calves, may occasionally pose a risk to walkers with dogs. If you ever feel threatened by cattle, let go of your dog's lead and let it run free. Always bag and bin dog poo, or take it home.

Enjoying the countryside responsibly

Enjoy the countryside and treat it with respect to protect our natural environments. In Scotland, you can enjoy the outdoors on most land and inland water, as long as you act responsibly and follow the Scottish Outdoor Access Code – www.outdooraccess-scotland.scot.

The Scottish Outdoor Access Code

Responsible access can be enjoyed over most of Scotland including parks, hills, moors, mountains and woods, beaches and the coast, lochs, rivers and canals, and some areas of farmland. The key principles are:

Take responsibility for your own actions

- park sensibly and do not create an obstruction
- take your rubbish home

Respect the interests of other people

- respect the needs of other people enjoying or working in the outdoors
- follow any reasonable advice from land managers
- on farmland, leave gates as you find them and keep to unsown ground, field edges or paths
- access rights do not usually apply to farmyards, but if a well-used path goes through a farmyard, you can follow it
- paths are shared with others – let people know you are coming so you do not alarm them, and slow down, stop or stand aside if needed

Care for the environment

- don't disturb or damage wildlife or historic places
- never light open fires, barbecues or fire bowls in dry periods or near to forests, farmland, buildings or historic sites at any time
- never cut down or damage trees

SHORT WALKS SHETLAND ISLANDS

ROUTE SUMMARY TABLE

WALK NAME	START POINT	TIME	DISTANCE
1. Lerwick town trail	VisitScotland iCentre, Lerwick	2hr	7km (4¼ miles)
2. Bressay: The Ward of Bressay	Bressay Pier	2½hr	9km (5½ miles)
3. West Burra: Kettla Ness	Duncansclett, near Papil	2hr	6km (3¾ miles)
4. St Ninian's Isle	Bigton	2hr	5.5km (3½ miles)
5. Scat Ness and the Ness of Burgi	West Voe beach	1½hr	5km (3 miles)
6. Sumburgh Head and Jarlshof	Sumburgh Hotel	2½hr	6km (3¾ miles)
7. Drongi Field from Westerwick	Westerwick	1½hr	5km (3 miles)
8. The Broch of Culswick	Culswick	2¾hr	6.5km (4 miles)
9. Staneydale Temple	Staneydale, on the minor road between the A971 and Gruting	1hr	2.25km (1½ miles)
10. Sandness Hill from Huxter	Huxter, near Sandness	3hr	8km (5 miles)
11. Muckle Roe and the Hole of Hellier	Little-ayre	1½hr	4.5km (2¾ miles)
12. Grind of the Navir and Eshaness	Eshaness Lighthouse	2½hr	5.5km (3½ miles)
13. Ronas Hill from Collafirth Hill	Collafirth Hill, near North Collafirth	3hr	6.5km (4 miles)
14. Unst: Framgord	Hannigarth	1½hr	4.5km (2¾ miles)
15. Unst: Hermaness	Hermaness car park above the Shore Station	3hr	8.5km (5¼ miles)

MAP KEY

HIGHLIGHTS
wick old town, clifftop views, broch and loch
Ferry trip, views, highest point of Bressay
autiful bay, remote island, abandoned village
Sand tombolo, clifftop views
cenery, narrow rocky scramble, Iron Age fort
Seabird colonies, views, archaeological site
Sea cliffs, bays, island views, seabirds
Lochs, magnificent sea cliffs, broch
Important archaeological site, wildflowers
Viking watermills, views, hill summit
Beaches, sea cliffs and blowhole
tacular coastal scenery, cliffs, blowholes, lochs
ghest hill in Shetland with panoramic views
autiful sandy beach, abandoned Viking village
Moorland, sea cliffs, seabird colonies

SYMBOLS USED ON ROUTE MAPS

S — Start point

F — Finish point

SF — Start and finish at the same place

4→ — Waypoint

~ — Route line

MAPPING IS SHOWN AT A SCALE OF 1:25,000

0 KM   0.25   0.5
0 miles   0.25

DOWNLOAD THE GPX FILES FOR FREE AT

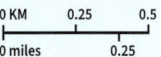
www.cicerone.co.uk/1194/gpx

Sea cliffs at Culswick (Walk 8)

INTRODUCTION

Looking south over the Bay of Deepdale (Walk 10)

The Shetland Islands are the remotest outpost of the British Isles, and some would argue they are the most beautiful corner too. These islands lie far out in the North Atlantic, closer to Norway than they are to Scotland, and give the visitor a wild experience and a sense of the adventurous. The biggest island of the group, known simply as Mainland, stretches from the stunning cliffs of Sumburgh Head in the south to the untamed beaches and rocky bluffs of Fethaland in the north, while between these two extremes the coastline takes in hundreds of miles of ragged headlands and large fjord-like inlets, known as 'voes' to the Shetlander.

Studding the sea around Mainland there are countless other islands too, many of which are inhabited. Everywhere you go on Shetland there is a myriad of wildlife to delight you, while the coastal scenery is wild and breathtaking.

Walking on Shetland

Much of the walking on Shetland is coastal, and it is usually pretty easy to find your way as often you just have to keep the sea to your left or right. The ground underfoot can vary from short, wind-scoured grassland to heather moorland or rocky clifftop. Many of the walks follow paths, and there is some

SHORT WALKS SHETLAND ISLANDS

waymarking in place for the most popular walks, but this is the exception rather than the rule. Generally route-finding is easy, though, and those routes that are pathless just follow the coast so you're not going to get lost. Where walks take you along the tops of sea cliffs, these are usually unfenced, so care is needed.

On any coastal walk you're likely to see spectacular arches and pinnacles of rock called stacks, and the coastline is indented with small rocky inlets known locally as 'geos'.

All the walks in this book are circular or out-and-back routes. Nine of the walks are on Mainland, but there are also walks on the smaller islands of Bressay, West Burra, St Ninian's Isle, Muckle Roe and Unst. Getting to both Bressay and Unst involves catching ferries (two to reach Unst via the island of Yell), while West Burra and Muckle Roe are both connected to Mainland by bridges. St Ninian's Isle is connected by a perfect example of a tombolo – a narrow spit of sand with the sea lapping on both sides – an adventure in itself!

Special things to see

Shetland is packed with amazing things to see. Probably the most immediately obvious, whether you arrive by sea or by air, is the stunning coastline. Here there are massive sea cliffs, deep voes, sheltered bays, islands, skerries, and some of the finest white-sand beaches in the world.

Adding colour and excitement to the coast is the wildlife. Shetland's shores are home to some of the world's most important seabird colonies, and

A fabulous puffin at Hermaness on Unst (Walk 15)

BASES AND PLACES TO STAY

in the summer months it is impossible to go to any sea cliff here and not see birds. Puffins, fulmars, guillemots, black guillemots, razorbills, kittiwakes and gannets fill the skies and the rocky ledges, and shingle beaches hold huge numbers of Arctic and common terns. The moorlands are the breeding ground for great and Arctic skuas, while red-throated divers nest on the hundreds of freshwater lochs inland. Common and grey seals are easy to see, and otters are abundant too. For many visitors their first sighting of that diminutive yet charismatic beast, the Shetland pony, will be memorable, and these can be seen all over the islands.

Shetland is very important geologically, and for this reason in 2009 it was designated a UNESCO Global Geopark. It is also justly famous for its archaeology – and while it doesn't have quite the abundance of historical sites that its neighbour Orkney can boast, what Shetland does have at Jarlshof, Clickimin, Scatness and the Ness of Burgi is just as important.

Bases and places to stay

Lerwick and Scalloway are the main towns in Shetland, and Lerwick in particular has a wide range of accommodation options, from a campsite and hostels to B&Bs, guesthouses and hotels. There are several other, more remote hotels scattered around Shetland, including at Sumburgh, Spiggie, Busta and Burrastow. Another good option for a budget holiday is the range of böds which can

Lerwick town centre from Victoria Pier

SHORT WALKS SHETLAND ISLANDS

be found around the islands – these are hostels managed by the Shetland Amenity Trust offering basic facilities with bedrooms, cooking facilities, toilets and a sitting area.

Getting there and around

Overnight ferries to Shetland ply between Aberdeen and Lerwick, taking around 12–13 hours, with a few a week going via Kirkwall in Orkney. Shetland is serviced by direct flights from Glasgow, Edinburgh, Aberdeen and Inverness, with all flights coming into the airport at Sumburgh on the southern tip of Mainland.

Once on Shetland getting around is relatively easy. There is a good bus network throughout the islands on all major roads, although getting to the more remote corners of Shetland, including some of the walks in this book, requires a car. The road network is superb, and cars can be hired in Lerwick or at Sumburgh airport.

For inter-island travel the Shetland Islands Council runs a very usable ferry service, with regular sailings throughout the day at an affordable price.

Looking towards Compass Head from Sumburgh (Walk 6)

WALK 1
Lerwick town trail

Start/finish	VisitScotland iCentre, Market Cross, Lerwick
Locate	ZE1 0LU ///palm.dragon.defectors
Cafes/pubs	Lots of options in Lerwick
Transport	Regular buses from Viking bus station to Market Cross
Parking	Victoria Pier car park, just across the road from Market Cross
Toilets	On the Esplanade, opposite Victoria Pier

Time 2hr
Distance 7km (4¼ miles)
Climb 95m

An easy walk around the old town of Lerwick, taking you round a spectacular coastal headland to the site of an ancient village

A superb introduction to everything Shetland. Starting at the tourist information centre, this easy walk on pavements throughout takes you through the beautiful old town of Lerwick, and along the coast to a rocky peninsula with amazing views out to the island of Bressay and along South Mainland. You then visit the ancient site of Clickimin Broch before returning via Fort Charlotte and the old town. A visit to the Shetland Museum, passed along the way, is highly recommended.

Clickimin Broch and the path leading to it

Boat on display at Shetland Museum and Archives

1 With the information centre behind you, facing the Market Cross, walk to the right along Commercial Street. Pass the Shetland Times Bookshop and cross over the A969 at the pedestrian crossing with the RNLI Shop to your left. Carry on along Commercial Street, passing The Lodberries on the left.

The Lodberries are houses backing onto the sea with a door giving direct access to the water. In 1814 there were 21 Lodberries along Commercial Street. More recently one was used as the home of Detective Inspector Jimmy Perez in the TV drama *Shetland*.

The Lodberries in Lerwick town centre

Looking out from the Knab

Commercial Street becomes Twageos Road. Continue along Twageos Road until you reach the entrance to the cemetery at **South Ness**. Follow a path on the seaward side of the cemetery wall, climbing uphill to a viewpoint and car park at **The Knab**.

2 From the car park go through a gap in the wall and follow a tarmac path along the bottom of the golf course, close to the cliffs but with a wall between you and the drop below. The path brings you out onto Breiwick Road. Turn left and follow the road to where it bends sharply right into Sletts Road and turns away from the sea.

3 Ignore the turn into Sletts Road, and instead follow a path on the left down by the shore. Keep on this path, with the sea to your left just over the wall, to reach South Road. Turn left and follow South Road, going straight ahead at the roundabout, using the crossing to the left. Opposite the petrol station on South Road, 280m from the roundabout, is a signpost for **Clickimin Broch**. Go through the gate onto the long straight path that leads to the broch itself.

Brochs are fortified round houses dating back around a thousand years and Clickimin Broch is one of many throughout Shetland. They are unique to Scotland, with the bulk of them being in Shetland and Orkney.

4 Walk back out onto South Road and turn right. After 160m take a right

WALK 1 – LERWICK TOWN TRAIL

down Westerloch Drive and walk around the back of **Clickimin Loch**, continuing on a track where the road swings to the left. Look for wintering wildfowl on Clickimin Loch, including tufted duck, teal, wigeon and whooper swans. At the far end of the loch pass Anderson High School on your left and reach Stanley Hill Road with the leisure centre to your right. Keep on Stanley Hill Road to North Lochside. Turn left, then second right into Anderson Road.

5 Walk up the hill to the end of Anderson Road and take a left at the T-junction. Go first right into St Sunniva Street and walk along this. Turn left onto Burgh Road and go downhill to the A969. Turn right onto Commercial Road and follow it to the mini roundabout.

Turn left here to visit the superb Shetland Museum and Archives nearby. This is the place to come to discover more about the human history, wildlife and way of life on the islands. There's a good restaurant inside, and you can see traditional boat building in action too.

6 From the mini roundabout continue along Commercial Road and just beyond the bus station fork right into Commercial Street, passing Fort Charlotte to your right.

Shetland Museum and Archives

SHORT WALKS SHETLAND ISLANDS

Fort Charlotte was built in 1665 to protect the Sound of Bressay during the Second Dutch War. It is an artillery fort, and was rebuilt in the 1780s during the War of American Independence, but never saw any action.

Continue along Commercial Street through the old town buildings, back to the Market Cross.

▬ To shorten

Make your way back to the Market Cross from any point on this walk by heading towards the centre of town and then downhill to Commercial Street.

A display of traditional rowing boats inside the Shetland Museum and Archives

WALK 2
Bressay: The Ward of Bressay

Start/finish	Bressay Pier at Maryfield
Locate	ZE2 9EL ///obstinate.erupted.wins
Cafes/pubs	Cafe and shop on Bressay near the marina
Transport	Ferry from Lerwick. No need to take a car
Parking	Victoria Pier car park in Lerwick
Toilets	At the ferry pier

Time 2½hr
Distance 9km (5½ miles)
Climb 245m

A wonderful, easy-to-follow walk up the highest hill on Bressay, giving magnificent views across to Mainland and the island of Noss

Bressay lies just across the Sound from Lerwick, and you can jump on a ferry there and start walking as soon as you arrive. The initial part of this walk follows the quiet public road along the shoreline, so is easy-going. The track to the summit of the Ward of Bressay is good underfoot, as it is the access road for the radio masts on the summit, so the whole route is easy to follow throughout.

The ferry that takes you to Bressay from Lerwick

The lighthouse on Bressay nestles beneath the Ward of Bressay

1 Follow the road from the pier, turning right at the T-junction at **Voehead**. At the next junction, keep right by the shore, and follow the road through **Voeside** and pass the marina to your right. Follow the road to the

The communication masts on the Ward of Bressay dominate the island

little chapel and cemetery, and turn left here, following the road to the crossroads by the shop.

2 Turn right down South Road, signposted Glebe and Kirkabister. After 2min come to a junction and keep left, carrying on along South Road with the Ward and its masts dead ahead. Keep on the road until you get to the village of **Glebe**. Pass a children's play park on the left, and immediately after this arrive at a junction, also on the left. This is Upper Glebe, the part of the village on the hillside.

3 Turn left and walk along Upper Glebe, continuing when the tarmac road becomes a track. Go over a cattle grid, through a gate and continue, climbing steadily on the good track. There are other tracks off to either side, but the main track is by far the most obvious, and you'll soon find yourself on the summit of the **Ward of Bressay** at 227m. There is a trig point tucked into a stone cairn.

> There are superb views from the summit across the Sound of Bressay to Mainland, and in the other direction over the eastern side of Bressay towards Noss. This island is a National Nature Reserve, and is especially important for its seabird colonies, particularly gannets.

4 Return to the ferry the same way.

> **– To shorten**
>
> For a shorter walk of 4km take a car over to Bressay and park at Glebe, walking from there (allow 1hr).

WALK 3
West Burra: Kettla Ness

Time 2hr
Distance 6km (3¾ miles)
Climb 160m

Stroll from the beach at Banna Minn to a deserted headland, with old crofts to explore and marvellous cliff scenery

Start/finish	Duncansclett, just along the road from Papil
Locate	ZE2 9LD ///improves.files.handfuls
Cafes/pubs	'Cake shed' 100m back along the road from the car park
Transport	No. 5 bus from Lerwick to Scalloway and onwards to Burra goes as far as Papil (800m from the start)
Parking	Small car park at Duncansclett
Toilets	No public toilets on route

An easy walk around a lovely headland, which is very nearly an island. Only the narrow spit, or tombolo, behind which the bay of Banna Minn nestles, keeps Kettla Ness attached to Mainland. The going is easy for the most part, with wind-cropped grass underfoot, although there are unfenced sea cliffs to be aware of on the west coast. Look for seals in the bay and wading birds on the beach. It's possible to include the walk up The Ward too, if you wish.

The tombolo that leads to Kettla Ness

23

The only building remaining at Minn on Kettla Ness

1 From the end of the car park go through the gate next to the large farm shed and follow the track downhill. You soon come to the tombolo with the beautiful white-sand bay of **Banna Minn** (often just called Minn beach) to your right. Drop down onto the beach and walk to the far end. The bay here is a great place to look for red-throated divers, particularly in rainy weather when they head to the coast to feed. Leave the beach and head up the hill to the cliffs at the far side of the headland, keeping the ruined croft houses of Minn off to your left. Reach the sea cliffs next to the rocky cleft of **Womni Geo**.

2 Turn left, keeping the sea to your right, and follow the clifftop along a small path in the grass. The cliff doesn't have a barrier, so take care as you go. Walk around the head of the bay and see the large rock pinnacle of **Fugla Stack** ahead. Keep going along the clifftop to reach the stack.

25

SHORT WALKS SHETLAND ISLANDS

Otter prints on Minn beach

As you walk there are great views along the coast, as well as out to the very remote island of Foula way out on the horizon. Looking the other way, back to Mainland, the Clift Hills dominate the view.

3 As you pass Fugla Stack climb a short way. Here you can make the short detour to The Ward, which at 58m is the highest point of Kettla Ness. Otherwise stay on the clifftop and continue to squeeze between the cliff to your right and the small lake of **Virda Vatn** to your left. Just beyond Virda Vatn go around the deep Spirls Geo and walk past Loch of Annyeruss. Move away from the sea cliff, and climb easily uphill to the trig point on **Grey Kame**.

4 From the trig point looking towards the Clift Hills on Mainland, you'll see a loch just 250m away. This is **Outra Loch**

The wonderful white sand at Minn beach

WALK 3 — WEST BURRA: KETTLA NESS

and is your next destination. From there walk leftwards, downhill to the **Bight of the Sandy Geos**, a lovely little bay. This is a great place to spot grey seals out in the bay, and further away into West Voe. Keeping the water of West Voe to your right, walk across easy grassy slopes to the first of the abandoned croft villages of Kettla Ness, **Gossigarth**.

The crofts on Kettla Ness started to be abandoned during the 19th-century Clearances, but some of the people remained here into the 20th century. There are some archaeological remains on the ness dating back 2000 years.

5 Explore the ruins then continue in the same direction to the village of **Minn**. From there head back to the tombolo, and either walk back along the top of the shingle spit, or back along the sandy beach if you prefer.

— To shorten

Enjoy the walk out to the cliffs at Womni Geo, then return. This shortens the walk to 2km (1hr).

The famous St Ninian's Isle tombolo (Walk 4)

Bigton village seen across the tombolo

WALK 4
St Ninian's Isle

Time 2hr
Distance 5.5km (3½ miles)
Climb 170m

A fabulous walk across a famous sand tombolo, followed by exciting clifftop views once on the island

Start/finish	Beach car park below Bigton
Locate	ZE2 9GA ///tower.occupiers.fountain
Cafes/pubs	None on route, shop in Bigton
Transport	Buses no. 6 and then 7 from Lerwick to Bigton
Parking	Car park down the hill from Bigton, overlooking the beach
Toilets	In Bigton opposite the shop (500m back along the road from the car park)

A memorable walk across the amazing sand tombolo, with the waves gently lapping on either side, followed by a circuit of the clifftops on St Ninian's Isle. The tombolo is a 600m sand spit, which can feel pretty exposed in rough weather, and the clifftops on the island are unfenced, so care is needed. The walk is easy, although there may be some boggy sections here and there after rain.

St Ninian's Isle from the car park

31

The ruins of St Ninian's Chapel

WALK 4 – ST NINIAN'S ISLE

1 At the bottom of the car park there are some useful information boards about St Ninian's Isle. Read these before heading down onto the sandy beach. Walk across the tombolo with **St Ninian's Bay** to your left and Bigton Wick to your right, looking in the sea either side for seals and maybe the occasional diver.

> The three species of divers you are most likely to see here are red-throated, black-throated, or great northern. In North America a diver would be known as a 'loon', while here in Shetland it would be a 'rain gus'.

On the far side a sandy slipway leads onto the island. Go up the slope, then turn right on a path across the grass to reach the site of **St Ninian's Church**.

2 From the remains of the church keep the sea to your right and walk across grassland on top of the cliffs to pass the jutting headland of **Scarfi Taing**. In Shetland 'scarf' is the local name for the seabird the shag. The shag's bigger cousin is the cormorant, known here as a 'muckle scarf'. The path takes you through a stone wall onto the narrow headland of **Loose Head**, with its trig point 59m above the sea.

3 Keeping the sea to your right, turn and walk southwards around the bay of The Neapack and along to the rocky inlet of **Selchie Geo**. The rocky islands off the coast are Fora Stack and Hich Holm and give great opportunities for a photograph. Keep walking on a grassy path to cross a stream, then lose height as you approach a narrow sea channel with the island of **Sweyn Holm** across the way.

4 Now turn to the left and follow the obvious path, again with the coastal cliffs to your right, for 300m before the path leads away from the coast and back to the tombolo. Cross and return to the car park.

> ⓘ *Shetland was known by the Vikings as Hjaltland and is a sub-arctic archipelago in the North Atlantic between the UK, Norway and the Faroe Islands.*

▬ To shorten
Stroll over the tombolo to see St Ninian's church, then return the same way. Gives a walk of 2km (1hr).

Looking back across the tombolo from St Ninian's Isle to Mainland

St Ninian's Isle

St Ninian's Isle was once tidal, but now you can walk across the isthmus to get onto the island. The isthmus, or 'tombolo' is a shingle spit covered by a deep layer of sand. This makes it unique in Britain, as all the others consist of exposed shingle or gravel. The island is named after the 12th-century church of St Ninian. Historians believe that the church was originally a house dating to the 1st century BC. When the ruin we see today was excavated in the 1950s, a local schoolboy discovered a larch box containing 28 pieces of Pictish silver.

ⓘ *Mainland has a total area of 967km² (373 square miles), which makes it the fifth largest island in the British Isles.*

WALK 5
Scat Ness and the Ness of Burgi

Start/finish	West Voe beach car park
Locate	ZE2 9JD ///stray.mourner.bleat
Cafes/pubs	None on route
Transport	Bus no. 6 from Lerwick
Parking	West Voe beach car park
Toilets	No public toilets on route

A good walk for seeing wildlife, and for enjoying the views across West Voe of Sumburgh to Sumburgh Head, and across the sea to distant Fair Isle. This otherwise easy walk does have a bit of a sting in its tail – to reach the Ness of Burgi with its hill fort you need to cross a narrow neck of rock, but there is a chain to hold onto and it's definitely worth the effort.

Time 1½hr
Distance 5km (3 miles)
Climb 50m

An easy walk along a peninsula to an Iron Age fort with fabulous views to Sumburgh Head, and to Fair Isle on a clear day

Ruined crofts near Loch of Gards

35

Fitful Head seen from the coast on the walk to the Ness of Burgi

1 From the West Voe beach car park go out onto the road and turn left. This is a busy road, so take care. Walk up the hill on the roadside, then down the other side to where the road bends to the right. On the bend there is a junction, signposted 'Scatness' to the left, which you should take. Follow this little lane between the houses of **Scatness** and on until the road ends just beyond a turning circle. There is a gate here that leads onto a continuation track.

2 Go through the gate and follow the track, with the **Loch of Gards** off to your right, with the mass of Fitful Head, the big hill in the distance, dominating the view in that direction. This is a good place to look for terns and

37

Looking towards Horse Island from the Ness of Burgi Fort

nesting wading birds in the summer, while in winter you might see ducks such as wigeon and teal. The track continues into a slight dip, then climbs gently out the other side and peters out, but there is a path through the grassland which takes you to the coast at a rocky geo. Just beyond this the headland narrows and becomes bouldery. Cross the boulders to gain the grassy path again, and in a short distance come to another narrow neck of land. This one is rocky and has a chain for you to hold onto for extra security. Once over this section you find yourself on the lovely **Ness of Burgi**. The path leads across easy grass to the ancient fort.

The Ness of Burgi Iron Age Fort is a low, fortified house that sits squat on the east side of the headland. Twin ditches lead to the house and you can crawl through the low doorways to gain entry.

3 Once you have explored the fort and enjoyed the views from the headland, walk to the end of the peninsula and follow the coast with the sea to your left, then return to the start by retracing your steps across the rocky section and back along the track to Scatness.

— To shorten

It is possible to squeeze a car along the road beyond Scatness. This will save having to walk along the main road and reduces the distance to 3km (1hr). Make sure you park sensibly and do not park in the turning circle.

The rocky section protected by a chain on the way back from the Ness of Burgi

The Sumburgh Head Lighthouse

WALK 6
Sumburgh Head and Jarlshof

Start/finish	*Sumburgh Hotel*
Locate	*ZE3 9JN ///tummy.relegate.spirit*
Cafes/pubs	*Hotel at start*
Transport	*Bus no. 6 from Lerwick*
Parking	*Sumburgh Hotel car park*
Toilets	*At Grutness Pier (210m off route)*

Time 2½hr
Distance 6km (3¾ miles)
Climb 220m

The impressive seabird cliffs at Sumburgh Head, and the chance to visit the most important archaeological site in Shetland

This walk should be right at the top of your list of things to do in Shetland. Start by visiting Jarlshof (entry fee applies), an exciting archaeological site dating back 4000 years, then enjoy spectacular coastal views as you walk up to Sumburgh Head. Here the RSPB have a nature reserve, and in the summer you'll see huge numbers of seabirds. The return takes you over Compass Hill with its interesting landforms and great views from the summit over the whole of South Mainland.

Wheelhouses at Jarlshof prehistoric and Norse settlement

SHORT WALKS SHETLAND ISLANDS

1 Jarlshof lies right next to the Sumburgh Hotel, and you can visit the site either at the start or the end of your walk, whichever suits you.

Explore the ruins then go back to the hotel car park through the gate down by the shore to pick up the path heading towards Sumburgh Head. The sea

Puffins at Sumburgh Head RSPB reserve

will be to your right throughout this walk. From the start look out for seals in West Voe, and perhaps even an otter down on the rocks. Keep close to the cliffs as you cross fields and stiles. As you approach Sumburgh Head the ground rises – climb uphill through a field to a stone wall where there is suddenly a jaw-dropping view down the cliffs into the sea, as seabirds wheel all about you.

> This is a great place to get the hang of seabird identification in the summer months. There'll be good numbers of guillemots and kittiwakes, and you will also see puffins and razorbills, as well as shags on the lower cliff ledges.

2 Follow the path around the cliff edge to gain the access road that goes up to the lighthouse on **Sumburgh Head**. You can explore the whole of the headland, looking over the wall at various points to watch the seabirds. Keep an eye out for passing whales out at sea – if you're very lucky you could see minke whale, orcas and other species here. Return to the **lighthouse** and walk back down the access road to a car park on a bend with a number of information boards on birds and whales.

> Sumburgh Head Lighthouse was the first lighthouse to be built on Shetland. It was designed by Robert Stevenson and constructed

Looking along The Slithers to The Compass

in 1821. It now houses a visitor centre, and a cafe in the summer months, but the light itself is still in use.

3 At the bend leave the road and climb uphill, steeply at first, with the rising sea cliffs to your right. Keep to the grassy path and soon reach the top of the hill. The slope to your right is a fantastic array of shattered blocks and landslides, known as The Slithers. Keep to the grassy path and continue to the top of **The Compass** with its large radar buildings.

4 Now walk down the access road for the radar buildings, following it downhill in a series of zigzags to emerge at a narrow public road at the bottom. Turn right and pass a small quarry on the right. Follow the road around the bend to the left and walk down to a T-junction in **Grutness**. The public toilets are 210m to the right here at Grutness Pier. Turn left at the junction and walk along the road back to the Sumburgh Hotel.

> **— To shorten**
>
> For a walk of 2km (1hr) drive up to the lighthouse car park on the bend in the road and just explore the area around the headland.

Jarlshof

Shetland's most important archaeological site, Jarlshof gives the visitor a glance back into a number of different periods in history. The earliest remains here are over 4000 years old, with wheelhouses of the Stone Age and Bronze Age. There are also Pictish and Viking remains that were built on top of the earliest ruins, and even the remains of a 16th-century laird's mansion house. Until 1905 the site was covered over by wind-blown sand and was only revealed by a tremendous winter storm that blew the sand away. Today the site is managed by Historic Environment Scotland and there is an entry fee (www.historicenvironment.scot).

ⓘ *The administrative centre of Shetland is Lerwick, but before 1708 the capital was Scalloway.*

Looking along the seacliffs southwestwards from Westerwick (Walk 7)

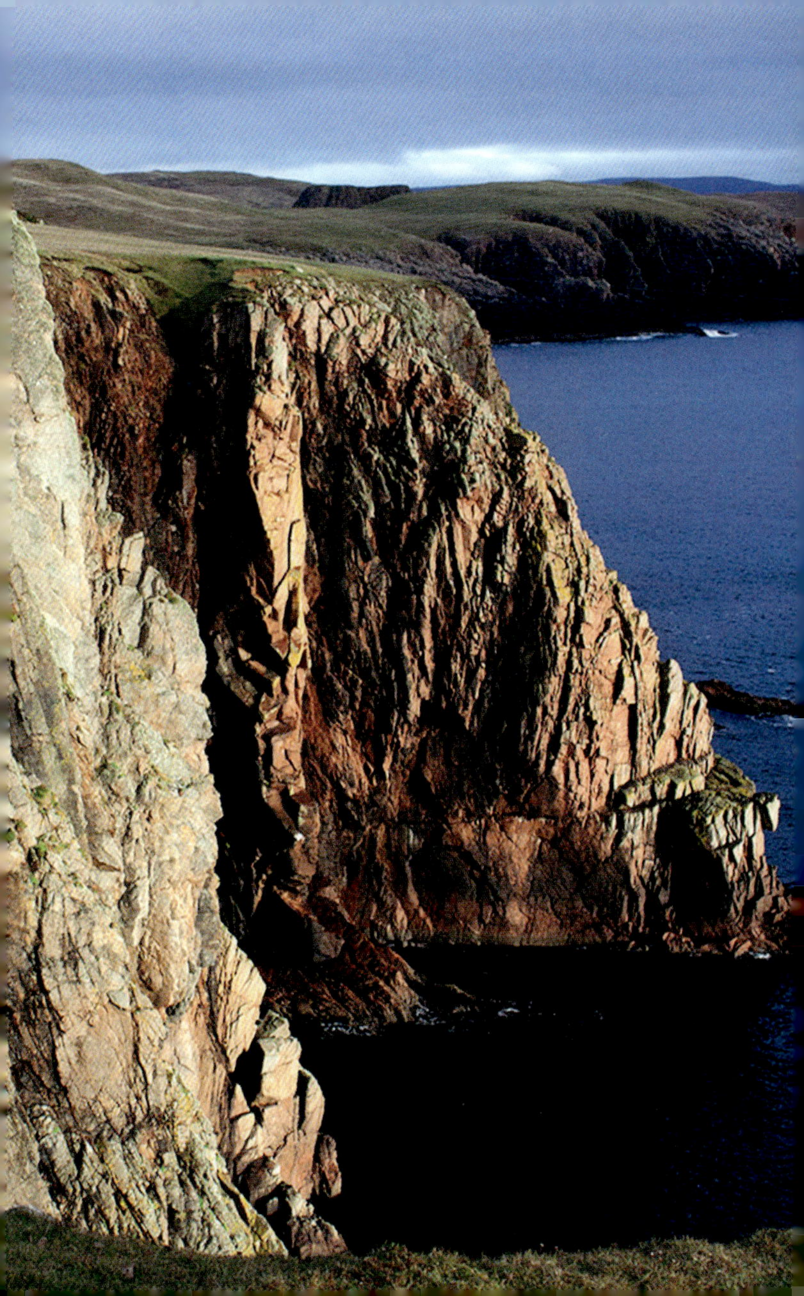

Stunning sea stacks at Wester Wick

WALK 7
Drongi Field from Westerwick

Start/finish	*Westerwick road end*
Locate	*ZE2 9NL ///rebounds.amaze.beard*
Cafes/pubs	*None on route*
Transport	*No public transport*
Parking	*Small pull-in at the end of the road in Westerwick*
Toilets	*No public toilets on route*

Time 1½hr
Distance 5km (3 miles)
Climb 220m

Superb views from a truly wild coastline, and an exciting walk close to magnificent sea cliffs

This is a route to savour. The clifftop walk is great for seeing seabirds and wildflowers, with views along the coast of Westside and South Mainland, and out to the islands of Vaila, Fair Isle and Foula. The walking is relatively easy on grassy slopes, but there are big unfenced drops into the sea on the coastal side, so care is needed.

The scattered village of Westerwick

SHORT WALKS SHETLAND ISLANDS

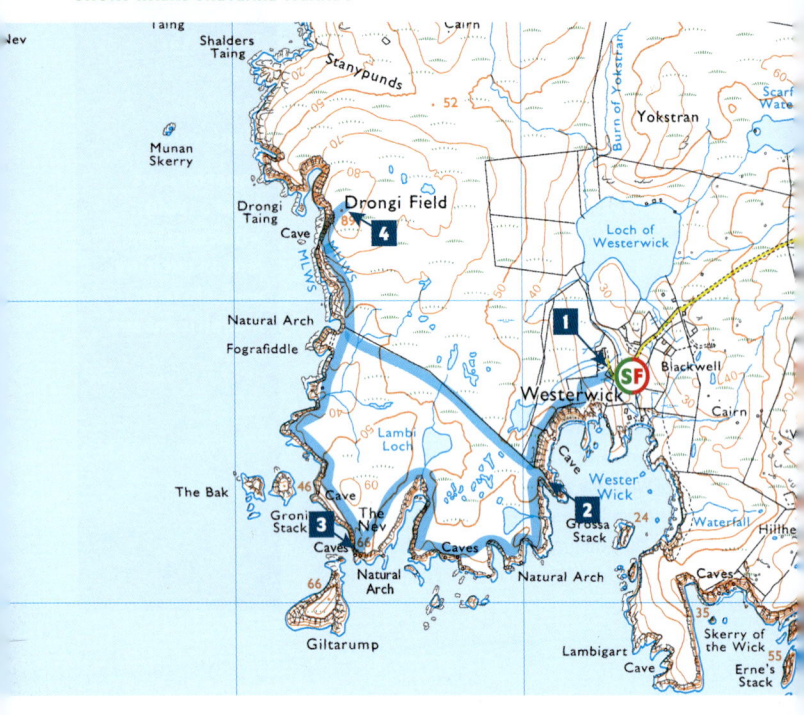

1 Just below the car park is a gate on the right that leads off the road and into a field. Go through the gate (making sure you close it behind you) and pick up a faint path through the grassy field to the far corner. The path leads to a gate that brings you out on the clifftop overlooking the bay of **Wester Wick**. The scenery here is impressive, with the rocky island of Grossa Stack out in the bay, and a narrow fang of rock splitting the bay in two. Go through the gate and turn right, keeping the cliffs to your left and a fence to your right. A steep little climb uphill takes you around the head of the bay to a fence corner, then across a stony section of ground to another fence.

2 After crossing the fence walk along the clifftop, crossing a stream that comes out from a small loch. This clifftop area is a great place to look for tiny wildflowers, such as moss campion, scurvy grass, spring squill and sea thrift. Continue down to a

WALK 7 – DRONGI FIELD FROM WESTERWICK

headland, then follow the coast round to the right, climbing over a small knoll to reach another little geo. Continue round impressive cliffs to the next bay, which is much larger than the last. Walk around the bay and at the back of it cross the little stream coming out of **Lambi Loch**. Now keep a little further away from the cliffs to your left and climb up grassy slopes to the top of the hill known as **The Nev**.

Islands dominate the view from here, including the impressive mound of Giltarump immediately offshore, and Groni Stack and The Bak off to your right.

3 From The Nev head a few metres further towards the clifftop and turn right, continuing around the coast, passing Groni Stack and The Bak. Continue downhill to cross a stream and look for a through-cave and natural arch in the next headland, **Fografiddle**. Just beyond this come to a fence. Climb the fence via the stile and follow the clifftop, climbing uphill gently to the summit of **Drongi Field**.

ⓘ *Of the 300 or so islands and skerries around Shetland, just 16 are inhabited, including Bressay, Unst and West Burra.*

Golden light on Drongi Field

The coast at Drongi Field

4 From Drongi Field head back to the fence. Cross back over, and turn left, following the fence all the way back to the edge of Wester Wick. Retrace your steps from here back to your car.

− To shorten

Follow the route as far as The Nev, then return to Lambi Loch and walk around to the back of the loch. From here head to the fence and turn right to Wester Wick and back to your car. This reduces the distance to 3km (1hr).

Seabird colonies

Although it is not one of the major nature reserve sites of Shetland, this coastline gives you the opportunity to see lots of birds. There are small colonies of kittiwakes and fulmars here, and you can also see guillemots and razorbills, as well as black guillemots. Look for rock doves – the true wild cousin of the ordinary pigeon! On the inland lochs you might see

WALK 7 – DRONGI FIELD FROM WESTERWICK

red-throated divers, as well as wading birds such as lapwings, redshanks, ringed plovers and oystercatchers. Further inland you might also see curlews and golden plovers, while this is one of the places in Shetland where mountain hares can also be found.

A fulmar or 'maalie' on Shetland

ⓘ *The recorded population of Shetland is around 23,000 people, although this does fluctuate during the summer tourist season.*

Remote croft houses at Culswick

WALK 8
The Broch of Culswick

Start/finish	The old telephone box, Culswick
Locate	ZE2 9NL ///fines.clicker.seemingly
Cafes/pubs	None on route
Transport	No public transport
Parking	By the barn after the track junction by the telephone box
Toilets	No public toilets on route

Time 2¾hr
Distance 6.5km (4 miles)
Climb 160m

An easy walk along a good farm track to an ancient dwelling on a magnificent clifftop, with fine views out to the island of Vaila

This route takes you to the ancient fortified dwelling known as the Broch of Culswick, a truly splendid setting for a house, with far-reaching views over the sea to the island of Vaila. It's an easy walk to start, following a good track almost all the way to the Broch of Culswick, then a clifftop walk to the stony beach at Sotersta, and an exploration of the old, long-abandoned crofting village there.

Looking towards Burga Stack

SHORT WALKS SHETLAND ISLANDS

1 Between the telephone box and the barn is a track that takes you gently uphill to a gate leading to Culswick Wesleyan Methodist Church. Ignore the track through the gate on the left and follow the obvious track to the right by the church. There's a second track, on the right this time, that leads up to the church, and you should ignore this too. Continue on the main track, which passes between a cluster of ruined croft houses then descends to cross a stream. Pass through a gateway and cross another stream, before coming to the shores of **Loch of Sotersta** on your left.

Loch of Sotersta is a good place to see a range of duck, geese and swan species, especially in the winter months. Look for whooper swans here, as well as greylag and Canada geese, wigeon and teal.

2 Keep to the track around the loch. As the track moves away from the loch shore, gaining height slightly, reach a track junction. You will come back to this junction later on your return route.

3 Go straight ahead at the junction, then bend to the right to reach the shores of **Loch of the Brough**, another good wildlife spot. The track begins to fade underfoot, and a path on the left leads to the outflow of the loch. Here you'll find a wonderful old manmade causeway, probably dating back to the days when the Broch of Culswick was lived in. Carefully pick your way across the stony causeway,

The Loch of Sotersta at sunset

WALK 8 – THE BROCH OF CULSWICK

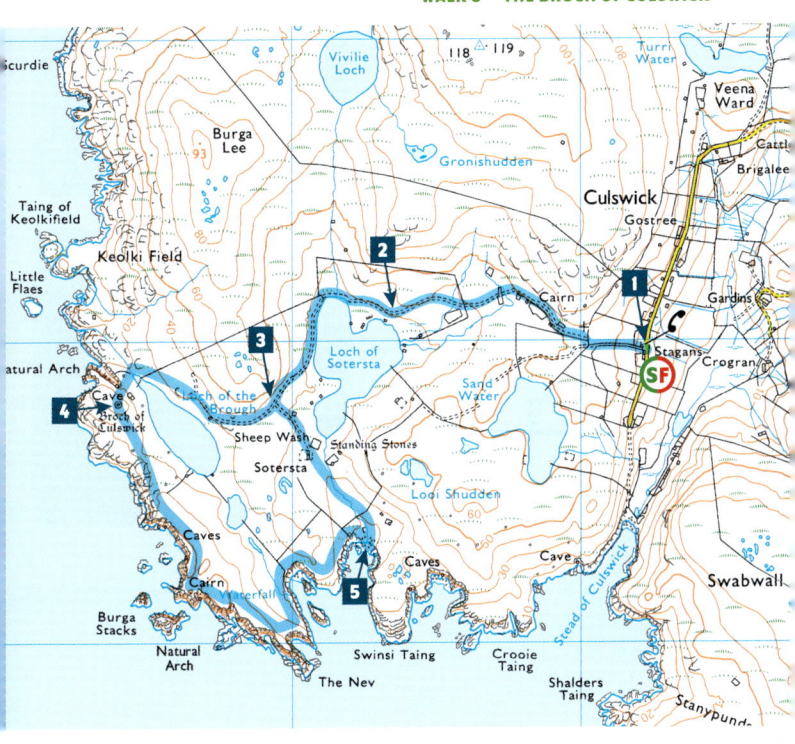

then go through a gate and up the grassy slope dead ahead to the rocky knoll, passing a ruined croft house. The rocky knoll is a man-made pile of rocks and is the ancient **Broch of Culswick**.

The ruined Broch of Culswick is an example of a fortified dwelling place typical of the north of Scotland, dating back to the 1st century BC. The views to Vaila and Foula from here are fantastic.

4 From the broch turn left, with the sea to your right, and follow the coast, with the sea cliffs rising impressively as you go. Reach a little knoll right on the cliff edge with a cairn on top, with great views of the **Burga Stacks** just off shore. Keep going around the clifftop, descending slightly to the

SHORT WALKS SHETLAND ISLANDS

twin-headland of **The Nev**, then continue walking around the headland to the stony beach at Sotersta.

5 From the back of the bay climb the grassy bank and follow the stream inland to the old village of **Sotersta**, where you'll find ruined croft houses, as well as 'plantie crubs'. These small, circular enclosures made of drystone walling were used to grow vegetables, and offer protection from the wind, as well as sheep and rabbits. At Sotersta you'll reach a track. Follow this to the track junction passed earlier on your walk (Waypoint 3). Turn right and follow your outward route back to the start.

> **− To shorten**
>
> Go there and back to the broch along the track for a walk of 4.5km (1hr 30min).

> **+ To lengthen**
>
> Instead of heading inland from the beach at Sotersta (Waypoint 5), follow the coast all the way round to the Stead of Culswick. Here a track leads up to the road end, and you can follow this back to your car. Total distance 7km (3hr 15min).

Looking back towards the Broch of Culswick

WALK 9
Staneydale Temple

Start/finish	*Sign for Staneydale Temple on the minor road between A971 and Gruting*
Locate	*ZE2 9NR ///stew.ferrying.callers*
Cafes/pubs	*None on route*
Transport	*No public transport*
Parking	*Roadside parking by sign. This is a passing place so park carefully at one end*
Toilets	*No public toilets on route*

Time 1hr
Distance 2.25km (1½ miles)
Climb 50m

A very easy inland walk through wildflower meadows and moorland to an important archaeological site

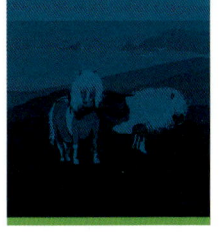

An easy, waymarked trail that takes you through lovely meadows and moorland to the site of a 5000-year-old village and its centrepiece, known as the Staneydale Temple. This is a great walk if you only have a short time and want to visit an important archaeological site, but it can be combined with other short walks nearby too. One of the best short inland walks in Shetland.

The entrance to Staneydale Temple

59

A walker exploring at Staneydale Temple

WALK 9 – STANEYDALE TEMPLE

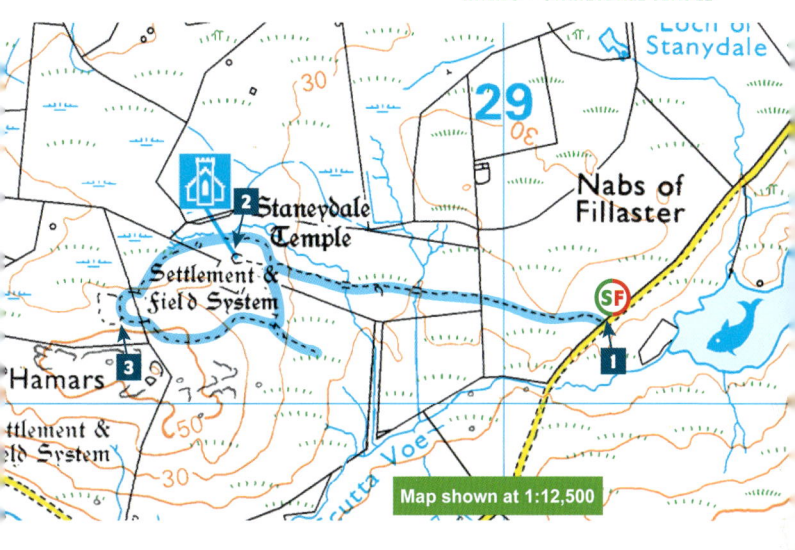

Map shown at 1:12,500

1 Go through the gate on the opposite side of the road from the sign. The path is easy to follow through beautiful wildflower meadows in the summer, if a little boggy in places, and there are waymarkers along the way. Go through a gate, then pass the outline of some Neolithic dwellings. Cross two streams and climb up to the **Stanleydale Temple**.

Staneydale Temple

SHORT WALKS SHETLAND ISLANDS

What we know as the Staneydale Temple is an oval measuring 14m by 10m. It is very similar to Neolithic houses of the period, but twice as large as any others on Shetland.

— To shorten
If time is really pressing walk to the temple and return without exploring the village site. Allow 30min.

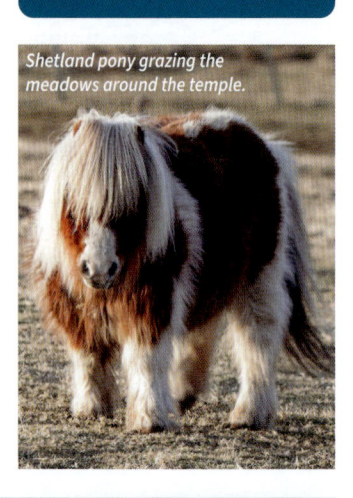

2 Return to the path that encircles the temple itself, turn right and follow it up the hill, making detours to visit other smaller remains. There are the remains of more Neolithic houses, each site marked by a stone cairn, as well as the outline of a field system. Walk through a gate in a fence to the highest point of the path.

3 Carry on around the path, back through the fence via another gate, then back to the path leading up to the temple. Now retrace your steps back to your car.

Shetland pony grazing the meadows around the temple.

Staneydale Temple

The origins of Staneydale Temple are puzzling. What we see is the only megalithic structure in Shetland from prehistory. It's an oval enclosure, made of large boulders, and would probably have had a timber roof. It could easily have been a courthouse, village hall, or chieftain's dwelling. Nobody knows for sure, but the archaeologist Charles Calder, who excavated the site in 1949, likened it to temples he had seen in Malta, so gave it the name we use today. Calder's excavation also revealed piles of burnt sheep bones and a Shetland Knife made of polished stone.

WALK 10
Sandness Hill from Huxter

Start/finish	Huxter near Sandness
Locate	ZE2 9PL ///twitches.housework.presses
Cafes/pubs	None on route
Transport	Bus no. 9 then 10 from Lerwick to Sandness, via Walls. Join the walk at Waypoint 5
Parking	Car park for Huxter Ancient Watermills
Toilets	No public toilets on route

Time 3hr
Distance 8km (5 miles)
Climb 300m

A fairly challenging walk up Sandness Hill, with extensive views from the summit and a pathless descent across wild moorland

This walk starts off easily enough and explores a series of Viking watermills on the edge of a stream. Then it heads for the heights of Sandness Hill, with views over the magnificent Bay of Deepdale, and a section of moorland walking leads to the summit at 249m. A short walk off the hill is pathless, but easy in good visibility, and soon you're on the road in Sandness village, heading back to the start.

The summit cairn and trig point on Sandness Hill

Banks Head sweeping into the Bay of Deepdale

1 From the car park the road you arrived on splits. Take the right-hand fork, passing the houses at **Huxter** to your left. Go through the gate on the left and follow the well-marked path to the Viking watermills.

The design is unique to watermills of the Viking period, being a shaft with paddles that turn horizontally. These are known as click mills from the sound they make when turned by water action.

65

SHORT WALKS SHETLAND ISLANDS

The workings of a click mill at Huxter

Click mills can be found throughout Shetland, Orkney and Lewis.

2 Go through the gate and follow the coast, with the sea to your right. The cliffs here are low, and you often get views of seals hauled out on the rocks. Keep along the coast to **Pund Head** and start to climb slightly. Off to your left is Loch of Skaaga. Walk between the loch and the sea cliffs, enjoying the views of Hesti Geo down to your right. Reach a fence just as the hill ahead starts to rear up.

3 Go through the gate in the fence and walk steeply uphill gaining views of the massive sweep of the Bay of Deepdale to the right. As the gradient eases leave the coast and follow a faint path up the crest of the hill ahead. Pass a small pond and soon after reach the

Walkers heading down the Burn of Mirdesgill from the summit

summit of **Ramna Vord**, with a cairn. Drop down the other side of the hill into a stony saddle, then climb out the other side to the summit ridge of **Sandness Hill**, with its twin summits. The first top has two cairns and is slightly lower than the next which has an ancient cairn and a trig point.

4 Head down from the trig point in the direction of Sandness. There's no path but you'll soon see the **Burn of Mirdesgill** ahead. Follow the right bank of the stream to reach a gate in a fence. Go through the gate and follow a flower-filled track to pass the Sandness Woollen Mill on your right just before you reach the public road in **Sandness**.

5 Turn left along the road and follow it back to the car park.

Moorland birds in the nesting season

Sandness Hill is a good place to see a range of birds typical of Shetland moorlands. Wading birds are fairly easy to see in the summer season, and here you'll find curlew, whimbrel, redshank, dunlin, golden plover and ringed plover. The ponds on Sandness Hill may have breeding red-throated divers, but it is illegal to disturb these (or any other bird for that matter) on the nest, so view from a good distance with binoculars. Arctic and great skuas can also be found nesting up here.

The coast near the lighthouse (Walk 11)

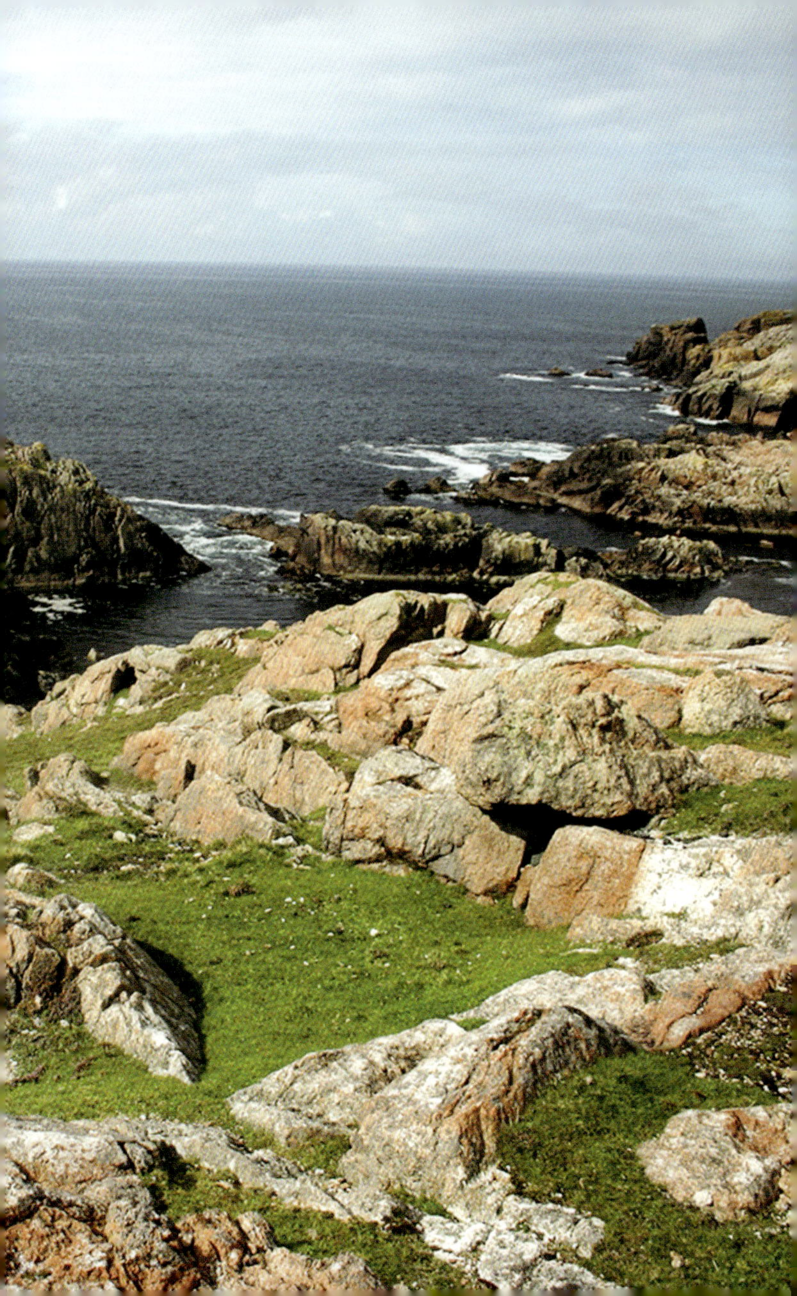

Enjoying the views of the Muckle Roe coast

WALK 11
Muckle Roe and the Hole of Hellier

Time 1½hr
Distance 4.5km (2¾ miles)
Climb 215m

Spectacular coastal scenery with lovely red granite sea cliffs

Start/finish	Little-ayre at the end of the public road on Muckle Roe
Locate	ZE2 9QW ///clearing.majors.soggy
Cafes/pubs	None on route
Transport	No public transport
Parking	Small parking area just back up the road from Little-ayre
Toilets	No public toilets on route

Connected to Mainland by a bridge, Muckle Roe (meaning big red island) is a superb place to visit. The walking here is beautiful and it's worth taking time to discover the whole island. While many visitors walk out to the Hams, this walk is shorter but no less spectacular. The going is on a good path for the most part, but a little off-path exploration is required at the lighthouse.

The path leading down to Gilsa Water

1 Go through the farm gate between the houses and follow a track across a field. Almost immediately the main track turns right and goes up the hill – ignore this and stay on the faint path that continues dead ahead and doesn't go uphill. Aim for a gate through a fence, after which the path becomes much more obvious and leads downhill to the gorgeous beach

Looking back at the beach at Muckle Ayre

The Muckle Roe Lighthouse

at **Muckle Ayre**. After exploring the beach cross the stream and follow the path uphill. The path takes a sharp left just as it gets steeper and brings you to a junction.

2 Turn right at the junction, going steeply up the short slope to come to the crest of **Burki Hill**. There are views to your left of the island of Vementry, with Papa Little to its left. Out on the horizon is Papa Stour. The path descends slightly to cross a stream, then contours around the flank of Brunt Hill before climbing up a short gully to a viewpoint overlooking the **Loch of Brunthill**. Keep on the path as it descends the other side towards the lovely little loch of Gilsa Water.

3 Cross the stream and come to a path junction. Take the path to the right, following the shore of **Gilsa Water**. Once you are level with the far end of the loch, turn sharp left and walk down a pathless slope to the coast. Now turn left again, so the sea is to your right, and follow the coast around to the tiny **lighthouse**.

4 Looking inland from the lighthouse the path starts again. Walk around a deep geo, then uphill slightly and round to the right. The path passes above the spectacular **Hole of Hellier**, and you may wish to deviate slightly from the path to have a careful peek into the huge hole in the ground.

The point where you cross the stream at Gilsa Water

The Hole of Hellier is what is called locally a 'gloup'. It is the remains of a sea cave whose roof has collapsed, leaving the hole. The name 'gloup' comes from the sound of the sea as it crashes into the hole.

5 Now regain the path and turn right, continuing up the hill. The path takes you over a rocky shoulder then bends round to the left, back to the stream at **Gilsa Water**. Go over the stream and retrace your steps back to your car.

> **– To shorten**
>
> Stroll to the beach at Muckle Ayre and back to the start for a short walk of 1km (30min).

> ⓘ *In the 1970s oil was discovered in the North Sea and this made a significant boost to the economy of these islands. Shetland is one of the richest councils in the UK.*

WALK 12
Grind of the Navir and Eshaness

Start/finish	*Eshaness Lighthouse, signposted off the B9078 before reaching Hillswick*
Locate	*ZE2 9RS ///obliging.sand.history*
Cafes/pubs	*None on route*
Transport	*No public transport*
Parking	*Clifftop car park on the right immediately before the lighthouse*
Toilets	*No public toilets on route*

Time 2½hr
Distance 5.5km (3½ miles)
Climb 90m

Easy access, unique coastal geology and breathtaking scenery make this a popular walk with visitors and locals alike

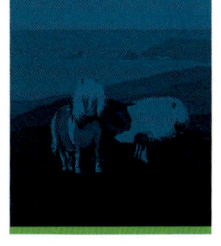

A very easy walk mainly over grass, with lots of interest throughout. It starts at the top of the huge sea cliffs at Eshaness Lighthouse, then takes in the Holes of Scraada and the Grind of the Navir, both superb examples of coastal erosion features, before a return along the cliff edge. There are paths most of the way, but none of the clifftops are fenced so great care is needed.

Looking back towards the Eshaness Lighthouse from near the Grind of the Navir

The Holes of Scraada

1 From the car park at Eshaness Lighthouse walk along the grassy clifftop, parallel to the road. Below you is a huge gulf, **Calder's Geo**. Walk to

Walkers on the clifftop near Calder's Geo

SHORT WALKS SHETLAND ISLANDS

the back of the geo to a little knoll. From here you get a great view down into the geo, and will see fulmars and black guillemots on their nests during the summer months.

> Calder's Geo is an example of a collapsed sea cave. The cave would have been created by water action at a weakness in the rock. Eventually the cave roof collapsed, forming a blowhole and an arch, then the arch also collapsed, leaving this geo.

2 Down the hill you will see a loch – head towards this down easy, grassy slopes, but without a path. Once you reach the **Loch of Houlland**, walk around the shore clockwise, crossing a wall via a stile. You will come to a little spit of land that juts into the loch, with the remains of a broch.

3 Just beyond the broch is a stream. Follow it past the remains of several Viking horizontal watermills, known as click mills, then continue along the stream until you reach the massive **Holes of Scraada**.

> The Holes of Scraada are a good example of a blowhole, a sea cave whose roof has collapsed. The name means 'The Devil's Holes', derived from an old word for the Devil – Old Scratch.

4 From the Holes of Scraada head for the sea and turn right along the top of the sea cliffs. Cross a number of stiles over walls and fences, and pass **Gruna Stack** off shore to your left. Just

The view back along the coast towards the Grind of the Navir

WALK 12 – GRIND OF THE NAVIR AND ESHANESS

beyond Gruna Stack come to an area of exposed rock on the left that looks remarkably like a man-made quarry but is actually cliff erosion. This is the **Grind of the Navir**.

5 Retrace your route back along the clifftops, but don't deviate when you near the Holes of Scraada. Instead stay beside the coastal cliffs. Cross a stream, then climb uphill slightly to reach two lochs, the **Lochs of Dridgeo**.

6 Keep between the lochs and clifftop, continuing around the coast until you can cut across the grassy top to the north side of Calder's Geo. Turn left to walk around Calder's Geo back along the road to the lighthouse.

> **– To shorten**
>
> Walk out to the Holes of Scraada (Waypoint 4) and return via the coast for a shorter 3.5km (1hr) circuit.

The Grind of the Navir

The Grind of the Navir

This remarkable cleft between two towers of rock is thought to have been created by a tsunami that ripped the cliff apart, leaving a deep trench in the seabed just offshore. The ocean currents here are huge, and the water tears rocks from the clifftop. These rocks are hurled by the water, and thousands of them can be seen way back from the cliff edge – some of them 100m or more – forming a raised boulder beach.

Walker on Mid Field summit

WALK 13
Ronas Hill from Collafirth Hill

CHALLENGE ROUTE

Time 3hr
Distance 6.5km (4 miles)
Climb 320m

A challenging walk to the summit of Shetland – one to save for a fine day, when the views all around will be far-reaching

Start/finish	By the radio masts on Collafirth Hill near North Collafirth
Locate	ZE2 9RX ///busters.preparing.laugh
Cafes/pubs	None on route
Transport	No public transport
Parking	Outside the radio mast enclosure, reached via a rough but driveable road from the A970 north of North Collafirth village
Toilets	No public toilets on route

A brilliant walk to the highest summit of Shetland. Ronas Hill feels like a mountain, despite its lowly size (450m at the summit), and it deserves respect. Although it's not the longest, this is the most challenging walk in this book, being over pathless terrain. Keep it for a clear summer's day when there will be far-reaching views, and lots of wildlife on the hill too.

Looking back towards the radio masts on Collafirth Hill

SHORT WALKS SHETLAND ISLANDS

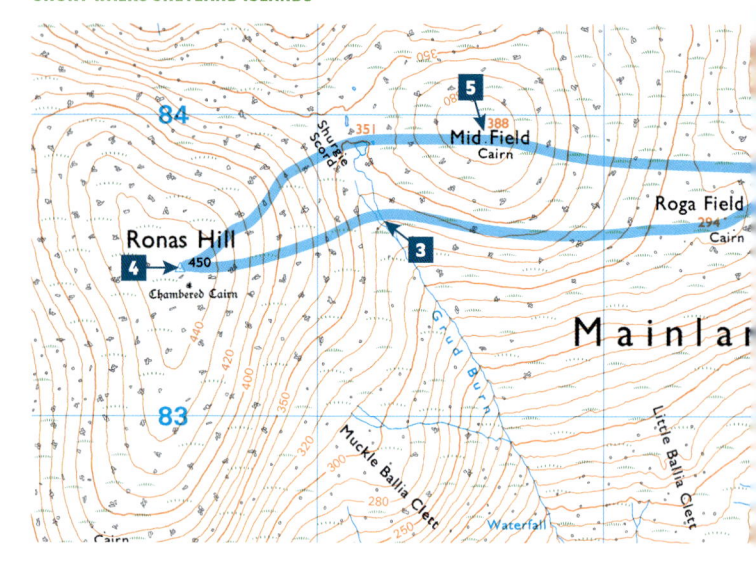

1 From the car park on **Collafirth Hill** you can see the higher hills to the west, Mid Field at 388m with Ronas Hill to its left at 450m. From the car parking area nearest to the bend in the access road, a faint path leads across a rough bouldery area to flatter grassland. Walk down to a saddle with a little

The view over North Mavine from the flanks of Mid Field

82

WALK 13 – RONAS HILL FROM COLLAFIRTH HILL

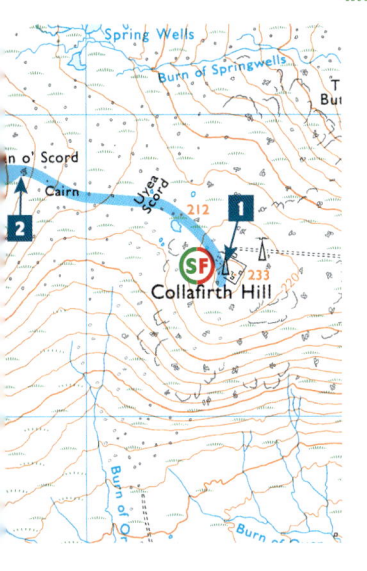

A mountain hare in its winter coat on Ronas Hill

pond known as Uyea Scord, then climb up the other side to a prominent rock, the **Man o' Scord**, just above a cairn. You will return to this point later in the walk.

2 Just off to the left, looking uphill, is a broad shoulder below Mid Field. Climb up rough slopes to this shoulder, known as **Roga Field**, where there is another cairn. Look out for the many Arctic Alpine plants that grow here, including the tiny-flowered trailing azalea and alpine lady's mantle. Ahead you'll see the flanks of Mid Field rising, which will be your return route, but for now go uphill, slightly left of Mid Field, skirting around the southern flanks to cross a stream, the **Grud Burn**, just below a saddle.

3 Ahead is **Ronas Hill**. There is no path, so just climb up the rough slopes until you reach the flat plateau that is the summit, marked by a trig point tucked into a stone shelter. There is a visitor book in a box for you to sign. Nearby is a huge Neolithic burial cairn of pink granite, which is said to be the resting place of the giant Ronas.

> The views from the summit of Ronas Hill stretch out to the huge sea cliffs of Eshaness to the south-west, and east to the Sullom Voe oil terminal. To the north-west you can see over the island of Yell to Unst.

4 Head downhill towards Mid Field, descending into the stony saddle at **Shurgie Scord** where you pass

SHORT WALKS SHETLAND ISLANDS

The ancient burial chamber on the summit of Ronas Hill

between two small ponds. Now climb out the other side to reach the summit of **Mid Field**.

This is a great spot to look for golden plover and ringed plover during the nesting season, and this whole area is one of the best places on Shetland to see mountain hares.

5 The masts on Collafirth Hill are visible ahead. Aim just to the left of that direction, down to the **Man o' Scord**, then retrace your outward route back to your car.

> ⓘ *There is a strong tradition and culture of story-telling and folk music in Shetland, and this continues to this day, with numerous festivals and smaller community events.*

WALK 14
Unst: Framgord

Start/finish	Road end at Hannigarth near Uyeasound
Locate	ZE2 9DL ///protester.cave.movie
Cafes/pubs	None on route
Transport	Ferry to Yell, then a drive across Yell and a second ferry to Unst (will add 4hr to your day if travelling from Lerwick). No public transport to start once on Unst
Parking	Small car park on the left at the end of the public road
Toilets	No public toilets on route

Time 1½hr
Distance 4.5km (2¾ miles)
Climb 80m

An easy stroll to the beautiful beach at Sand Wick and an exploration of the abandoned Viking village of Framgord

This is a lovely short walk onto one of Shetland's finest beaches. There are remains of a Viking longhouse to discover at the abandoned village of Framgord, and while the walk is short – suitable to squeeze in after a visit to Hermaness (Walk 15) if you wish – Framgord is well worth a visit in its own right and is a favourite picnic spot.

The view along Sand Wick to Framgord

SHORT WALKS SHETLAND ISLANDS

1 From the information board in the car park go over the stile and along the track towards the house at **Hannigarth**. Just before you get to the house go right over another stile and follow a faint grassy track downhill towards the sea. The beautiful bay at **Sand Wick** soon comes along – turn left and walk down onto the beach.

WALK 14 – UNST: FRAMGORD

2 Walk along the beach to its far end, gaining the grassy bank with the remains of the village of **Framgord**.

At Framgord you'll find a Norse longhouse, a byre which has an amusing cow-shaped doorway, and a chapel. There are also Pictish standing stones and burial mounds. The name Framgord comes from the Old Norse, and means 'furthest out farm'.

3 Drop down onto the back of the next beach, the **Wick of Smirgirt**, and go out onto the next headland, **Qui Ness**. The ruined village of Smirgarth lies on this headland.

4 Continue a short way into the bay of Burga Wick, then return the same way to Smirgarth and then Framgord. Go inland 50m or so and walk around the grassland above the beach to return to the path back to the car park.

> ⓘ *Fishing is still a big part of the Shetland economy, contributing a third of Shetland's economic output. In 2021 Shetland accounted for 12% of all the landings in the UK.*

The path to Framgord leads onto the beach at Sand Wick

A Shetland pony with its foal at Hannigarth (Walk 14)

WALK 15
Unst: Hermaness

Start/finish	Hermaness car park above the Shore Station.
Locate	ZE2 9EQ ///offers.rollers.attention
Cafes/pubs	None on route
Transport	Ferry to Yell, then a drive across Yell and a second ferry to Unst (will add 4hr to your day if travelling from Lerwick). No public transport to start once on Unst
Parking	Car park at the end of the B9086 road
Toilets	In car park

A superb circular walk at the very northern tip of the British Isles. Hermaness is the world's most important breeding ground for the great skua. As you reach the cliff edge you'll see – and smell! – the hundreds of thousands of seabirds nesting on this huge face, and gaze out to the gannetry on the island of Muckle Flugga. This walk is mainly on grass and wooden boardwalks and shouldn't be missed.

Time 3hr
Distance 8.5km (5¼ miles)
Climb 350m

A well-marked walk across the wild moorland at Hermaness to one of Britain's most important seabird breeding colonies

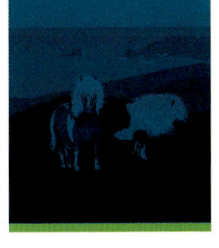

The Shore Station and car park at Hermaness

Map labels

Baa Skerries
Wilna Geo
Taing of Loosswick
Looss Wick
The Fram
Boelie
The Greing
The Fild
Humla Stack
Natural Arch
Clingra Stack
Urda Stack
Hermaness Hill
Flodda Stack
Herma Ness
Humlataes
Sothers Stack
Burn of Sournasdale
Stackingro
Long Sothers Kame
East Sothers Dale
Stackins-hocka
Raabit Kame
Kame of Flouravoug
Natural Arch
West Sothers Dale
The Fidd
Tooa Stack
Toolie
Sothers Brecks
Neapna Stack
Neap
Soorie Geo Cave
Yennastaba Dale
Saito
Hermaness National Nature Reserve
Burn of Winnaswarta Dale
Veedie
Fiska Geo
dda Kame
FB
Mill Fiel
Rutna
Mouslee Hill
Fiska Wick
Cleva N
The Ne
Cat Houll
P
Sheep Wash
SF
Lighthou
Shore Stat
Haila Leog
Boo Stacks
Lowerbulter
Sto
Upperbulter
Broch (remains of)
Burgar Stack

Negotiating the boardwalks across the boggy ground at Hermaness

1 There are information boards in the car park, which are well worth reading before starting the walk. At the far end of the car park is a gate leading to a good path. Follow this uphill, then through another gate to where the path traverses the side of a little gully. The path follows a fence then drops to cross a stream, the **Burn of Winnaswarta Dale**.

2 Once on the other side of the stream, turn left and keep on the path that runs parallel to it. Climb steadily onto an area of flat moorland, where there are wooden boardwalks to keep your feet dry as you cross the **Hermaness National Nature Reserve**.

If visiting in the summer you'll see lots of great skuas on the moorland. Known locally as 'bonxies', these large brown seabirds are very protective around their nesting areas. If you get too close to eggs or chicks the adults will dive-bomb you!

The Muckle Flugga Lighthouse from the Taing of Loosswick

Keep following the path, mostly grassy but occasionally on boardwalks where it gets boggy, across the flat moorland. Soon reach the edge of the huge sea cliffs. From the 1970s to the 1990s, the only black-browed albatross in the Northern Hemisphere, known as 'Albert', resided here among the gannets and other seabirds.

3 Turn right on the path that runs along the top of the cliffs, looking at the seabirds as you go. The clifftop is unfenced, so care is needed. Follow the path down into a gully and cross a stream. Now keep parallel to the coast, albeit a little bit further inland. It is a little boggy in places here. The white cliffs of the island of Muckle Flugga soon come into view ahead. The white cliffs aren't an indication of a change in rock type – they are thousands of gannets, known locally as 'solans', on their nests. Walk down the slope to a grassy headland called the **Taing of Loosswick**, which gives the best view of Muckle Flugga, with its lighthouse, and the furthest rock, known as Out Stack.

The lighthouse on Muckle Flugga was lit on 1 January 1858. It was built by Thomas and David Stevenson. Thomas was the father of the famous author Robert Louis Stevenson.

4 Climb back up from Taing of Loosswick and walk back the way you came for a short way to a signpost indicating a path going directly up the hill. Follow this path, steeply at first, then easing slightly as you reach the summit of **Hermaness Hill**.

WALK 15 – UNST: HERMANESS

Climbing the path up Hermaness Hill

5 Turn right at the summit and follow the path across boardwalks, over the moor and down into the gully where the **Burn of Winnaswarta Dale** is and regain the path you followed on your outward journey. Turn left here and follow the good track back to the start.

> **— To shorten**
>
> Follow the path up the Burn of Winnaswarta Dale to the seabird cliffs (Waypoint 3) and return via the same route. Total distance 4km (1hr 30min).

Hermaness

The headland is home to one of the world's most spectacular seabird colonies. In the summer months from late April until late July it is possible to see here all the iconic seabird species you would expect during a visit to Shetland. On the towering cliffs on the west coast you can get good views of guillemots, razorbills, black guillemots, puffins, shags, fulmars, kittiwakes and rock doves, while gannets fill the rock stacks offshore.

A gannet, or 'solan', at Hermaness

> ⓘ *The amazing Up Helly Aa fire festival takes place in Lerwick on the last Tuesday in January, with other events held throughout the islands around the same time.output. In 2021 Shetland accounted for 12% of all the landings in the UK.makes it the fifth largest island in the British Isles*

USEFUL INFORMATION

Tourism bodies

Visit Scotland
www.visitscotland.com
Promote Shetland
www.shetland.org
Visit Unst
www.visit-unst.com
RSPB
www.rspb.org.uk
Shetland Amenity Trust
www.shetlandamenity.org
Shetland Community Wildlife Group
www.shetlandcommunitywildlife.org

Tourist information centre

Market Cross, Lerwick
tel 01595 693434

Travel

Northlink Ferries
www.northlinkferries.co.uk
Shetland Island Council Ferries
www.shetland.gov.uk/ferries
Shetland buses
www.zettrans.org.uk
Bolts Car Hire
www.boltscarhire.co.uk
Star Rent a Car
www.starrentacar.co.uk

USEFUL INFORMATION

Glossary of common words in place names

broch	an Iron Age drystone walled fortified house
brough	similar to a broch, but the outer area or wall of a fortified house
geo	a rocky inlet on the coast
gloup	a sea cave whose roof has collapsed, forming a hole in the ground down to sea level, some way back from the cliff edge. The 'gloup' is the sound the sea makes as it is pushed through into the void
ness	a headland
voe	a sea loch/fjord
ward	a hill, usually an old lookout station
wick	a bay

Glossary of Shetland dialect words for wildlife

alamootie	storm petrel
bonxie	great skua
draatsi	otter
dunter	eider
horse-gok	snipe
longvie	guillemot
maalie	fulmar
muckle scarf	cormorant
neesick	harbour porpoise
rain gus	red-throated diver
sandiloo	ringed plover
scarf	shag
sea craa	razorbill
selkie	seal
shalder	oystercatcher
skooty allan	Arctic skua
solan	gannet
tammy norie	puffin
tirrick	Arctic tern
tystie	black guillemot

© Graham Uney 2024
First edition 2024
ISBN 978 1 78631 194 8

Printed in Czechia on behalf of Latitude Press Ltd on responsibly sourced paper.
A catalogue record for this book is available from the British Library.
© Crown copyright and database rights 2024 OS AC0000810376
All photographs are by the author unless otherwise stated.

CICERONE

Cicerone Press, Juniper House, Murley Moss, Oxenholme Road,
Kendal, Cumbria, LA9 7RL

www.cicerone.co.uk

Updates to this Guide

While every effort is made to ensure the accuracy of guidebooks as they go to print, changes can occur during the lifetime of an edition. Any updates that we know of for this guide will be on the Cicerone website (www.cicerone.co.uk/1194/updates), so please check before planning your trip. We also advise that you check information about transport, accommodation and shops locally. We are always grateful for updates, sent by email to updates@cicerone.co.uk.

Register your book: To sign up to receive free updates, special offers and GPX files where available, create a Cicerone account and register your purchase via the 'My Account' tab at www.cicerone.co.uk.